THIS BOOK
BELONGS TO
AN AWESOME
KID CALLED